Why Daily Handwriting Practice?

The premise behind *Daily Handwriting Practice* is simple and straightforward—frequent, focused practice of a skill leads to mastery and retention of that skill.

What's in *Daily Handwriting Practice*?

- The book is divided into 36 weekly sections. On Monday through Thursday students complete half pages to practice writing letters, words, and sentences. Friday's practice is a full page.

- A full-page chart showing proper letter formation is included.

- *Daily Handwriting Practice* is more than handwriting. While completing the handwriting exercises, students learn about a variety of curriculum topics:

The Alphabet	Unusual Animals
Capital Letters	Owls Are Amazing Hunters
Months of the Year	Whales
Days of the Week	The Water Cycle
Geography Facts	Using Good Verbs
Inventors	Figures of Speech
The Seven Continents	Colors and Alliteration
The Weather	Learning About Beavers
Our Presidents	Simple Machines
Games Around the World	Famous Quotations
Native American Tribes	Sports Around the World
Unusual Plants	Candy Around the World
Prefixes and Suffixes	Learning About Kenya
Rhyming Words	Writing About Math
Rivers of the World	Alphabets Around the World
Nonsense Rhymes	

Letter Formation Chart
Contemporary Cursive

Aa Bb Cc Dd

Ee Ff Gg Hh

Ii Jj Kk Ll

Mm Nn Oo Pp

Qq Rr Ss Tt

Uu Vv Ww Xx

Yy Zz

Daily Handwriting Practice • EMC 793

The Alphabet

Name:

Monday

a a a   cab
b b b
c c c   dab
d d d   brad
e e e   face
f f f   ace   bead
         fee   baa   deed

The Alphabet

Name:

Tuesday

g g g   kid
h h h
i i i   lid
j j j   bib
k k k   leg   hill
l l l   dig   jab
         big   cake

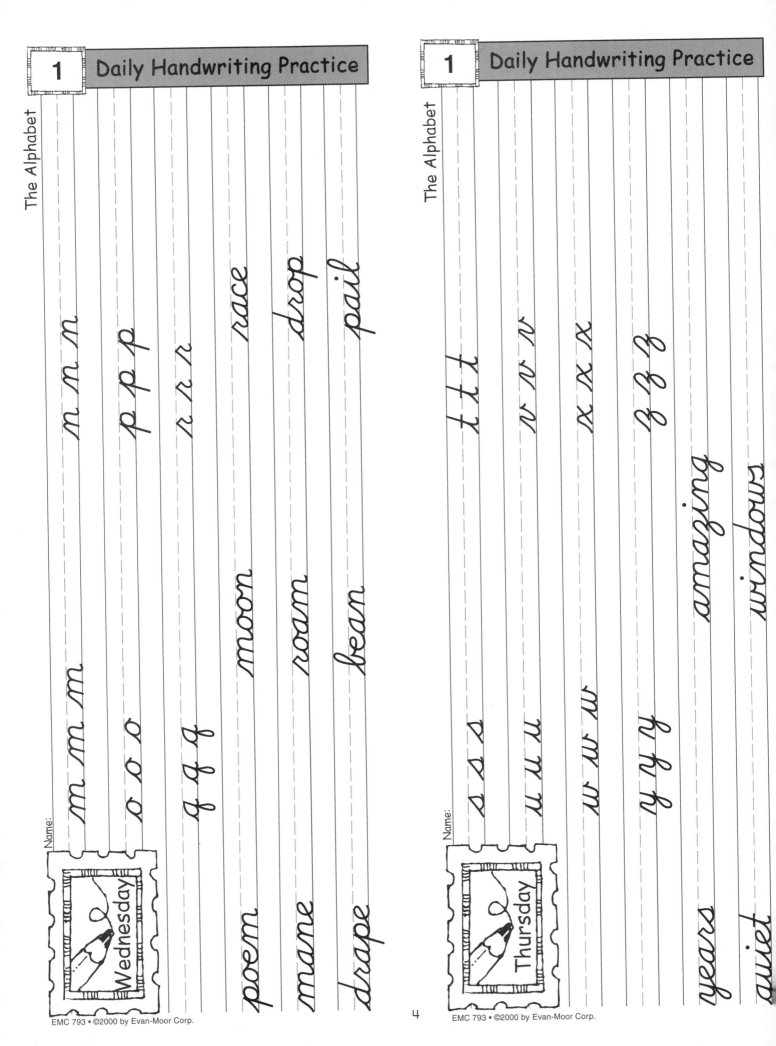

Name:

Wednesday

m m m
o o o
g g g

poem   moon   race
mane   roam   drop
drape   bean   pail

Name:

Thursday

s s s   t t t
u u u   v v v
w w w   x x x
y y y   B B B

years   amazing
quiet   quantum

Name: _____

Friday

In Just

when the world is puddle-wonderful

the queer old balloonman whistles far and wee

and betty and isbel come dancing

from hop-scotch and jump-rope and it's spring

e.e. cummings

e.e. cummings is a poet who uses very few capital letters.
Practice your lowercase letters by copying this stanza from his poem.

Sign your name like e.e. cummings. Use your first two initials and your last name with no capitals.

Capital Letters

Name:

Monday

A B C D E
F G H L
Bob
Dastri
Fran
Hoa
Gunter

Capital Letters

Name:

Tuesday

K L M N
O P R
Kanika
Maria
Olga
Raul
Jamal
Lama
Namid
Paul
Quon

Capital Letters

Name:

Wednesday

Scott
Usef
Walker
Xavier
Yasmin
Zeke

Capital Letters

Name:

Thursday

Aa Bb Cc Dd
Ee Ff Gg Hh
Ii Jj Kk Ll
Mm Nn Oo Pp
Qq Rr Ss Tt
Uu Vv Ww Xx Yy Zz

Name: _____

A Dialogue

Student: A, B, C, D, Eeee! A bee!

Teacher: No. A, B, C, D, E, F

Student: A, B, C, D, E, F, Gee, a bee!

Teacher: No. No. No.

Student: A bee!

Teacher: That's better. A, B, C...

Copy the letters and the words written in cursive.

Months of the Year

Months of the Year

Name:

Name:

Monday

Tuesday

January

February

March

Jumpin' January

Flag-waving February

Mixed-up March

April

May

June

Alarming April

Marvelous May

Jazzy June

Months of the Year

Name:

Wednesday

July

August

September

Jolly July

Ambitious August

Spirited September

Months of the Year

Name:

Thursday

October

November

December

Orderly October

Next-to-last November

Dazzling December

Name: _____

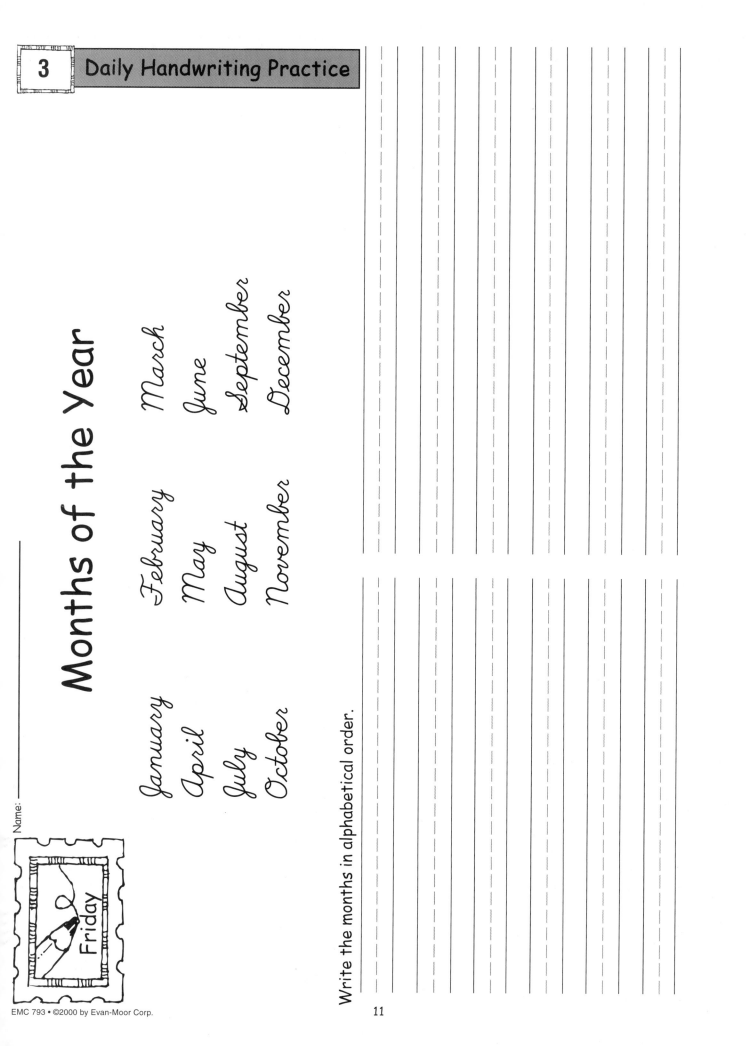

Months of the Year

January   February   March
April   May   June
July   August   September
October   November   December

Write the months in alphabetical order.

Days of the Week

Name:

Monday

Monday

Tuesday

Monday mornings make me merry.

Tuesday twilight turns into tomorrow.

Days of the Week

Name:

Wednesday

Tuesday

Thursday

Wild Wednesday winds whistle.

Thursday tornadoes turn treacherous.

Days of the Week

Name:

Wednesday

Friday

Saturday

Fun-filled Friday flies by fast.

Some summer Saturdays start slowly.

Days of the Week

Name:

Thursday

Sunday

swim

shower

Sunday's sun swims into showers.

Soon the showers slip back to sun.

Days of the Week

Name: _____

Friday

Monday's child is fair of face,

Tuesday's child is full of grace,

Wednesday child is full of woe,

Thursday's child has far to go,

Friday's child is loving and giving,

Saturday's child works for a living;

But the child that's born on Sunday

Is blithe and bonny, good and gay.

Copy this Mother Goose rhyme.

Name:

Monday

North   South

East   West

East is east and West is west.

But I think home is always best.

Name:

Tuesday

compass rose

legend

The compass rose shows directions.

The legend of a map is a key.

Name:

Wednesday

equator

prime meridian

These are imaginary lines on a map.

They help people describe locations.

Name:

Thursday

North Pole

South Pole

The North Pole is at the top of a globe.

The South Pole is at the bottom.

Geography Facts

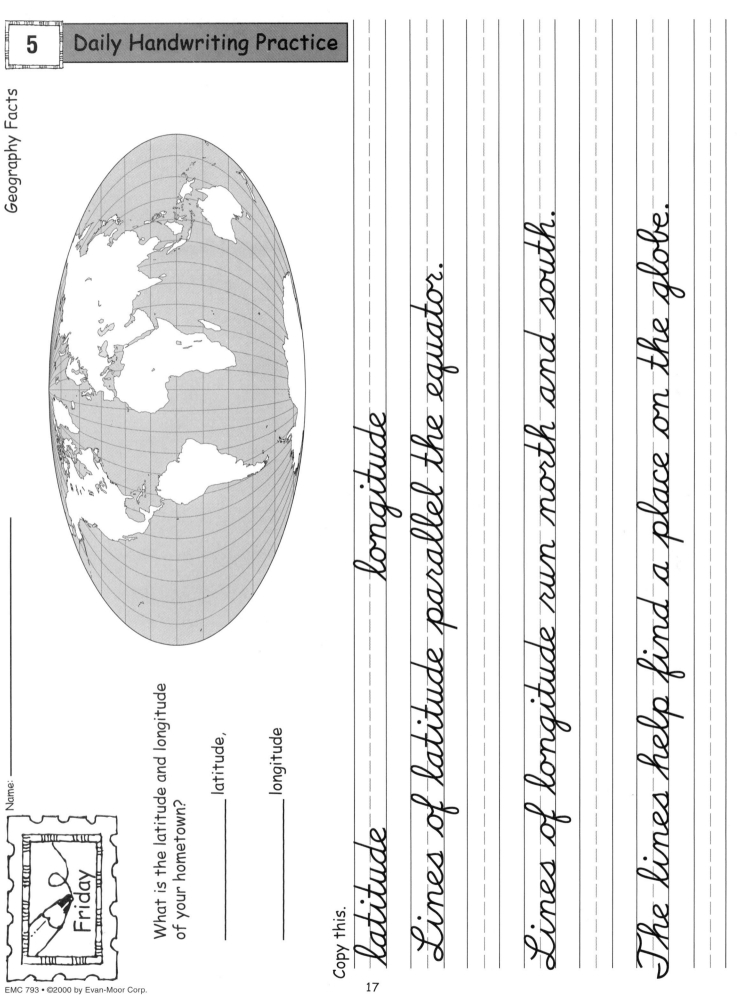

Friday

Name: _____

What is the latitude and longitude of your hometown?

_____ latitude,

_____ longitude

Copy this.

latitude

longitude

Lines of latitude parallel the equator.

Lines of longitude run north and south.

The lines help find a place on the globe.

Inventors

EMC 793 • ©2000 by Evan-Moor Corp.

Name:

Monday

telephones

A. G. Bell

Mr. Bell patented the telephone in 1876.

Today there are more than 425 million.

Inventors

(R. J. Anderson patented the idea of a washing machine with wooden tubs.)

Name:

Tuesday

washing machines

R. J. Anderson

People used to wash clothes by hand.

Then washing machines were invented.

18

EMC 793 • ©2000 by Evan-Moor Corp.

Name:

Wednesday

airplanes

Wright Brothers

In 1903 Orville flew for 12 seconds.

Today jumbo jets fly for many hours.

Name:

Thursday

automobiles

Henry Ford

Mr. Ford made Model T's in 1908.

Today computers help cars run well.

Name: _____

Friday

Famous Inventors

Jacques Cousteau .... SCUBA

Thomas Edison .... light bulb

Benjamin Franklin .... bifocals

Galileo Galilei .... telescope

Louis Pasteur .... pasteurization

George Westinghouse .... air brakes

Steve Wozniak .... personal computer

Copy the names of these famous inventors.

Jacques Cousteau

Thomas Edison

Benjamin Franklin

Galileo Galilei

Louis Pasteur

George Westinghouse

Steve Wozniak

The Seven Continents

Name:

Monday

continent

landmass

A continent is a large landmass.

The Earth has seven major continents.

The Seven Continents

Name:

Tuesday

North America

South America

is north of the equator.

is south of the equator.

Name:

Wednesday

Australia

Antarctica

These two continents are islands.

The South Pole is on Antarctica.

Name:

Thursday

Europe

Asia

Africa

Africa is the second-largest continent.

Asia is the largest and most populated.

The Continents

Name: _____

Friday

Write the name of each continent on the correct line.
Then answer the questions below.

Word Box

Australia   Antarctica
Asia   Africa
Europe   North America
        South America

1. _____
2. _____
3. _____
4. _____
5. _____
6. _____
7. _____

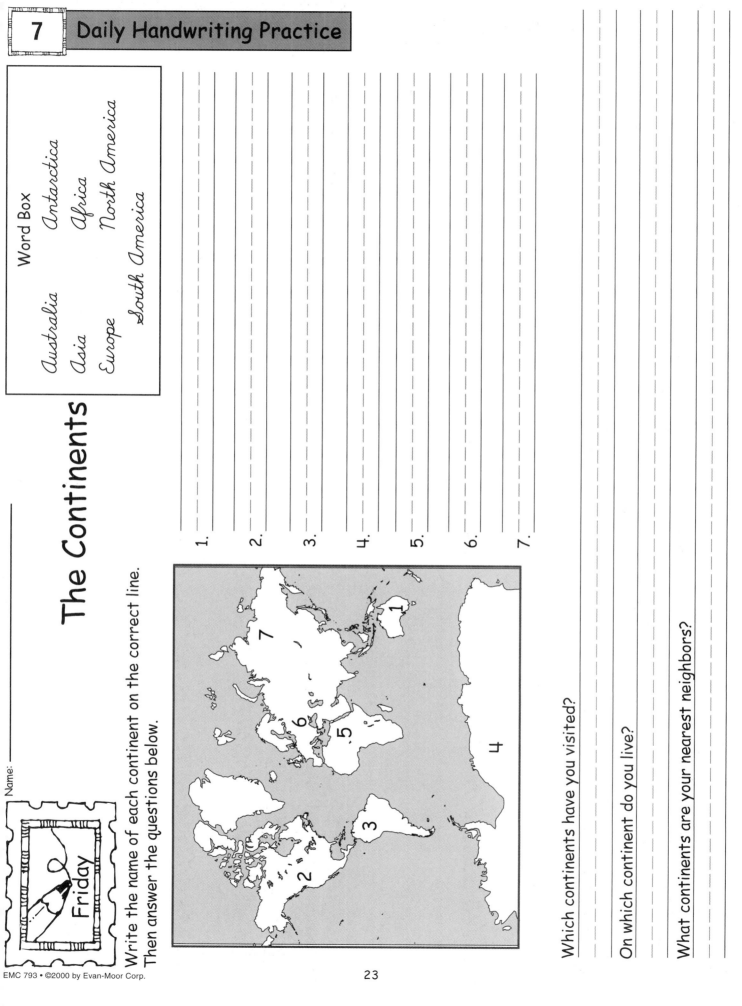

Which continents have you visited? _____

On which continent do you live? _____

What continents are your nearest neighbors? _____

The Weather

Name:

Monday

windy

rainy

sunny

snowy

cloudy

foggy

breezy

drippy

A weatherman gives a weather report.

The Weather

Name:

Tuesday

weatherman

meteorologist

A weatherman is a meteorologist.

When you give a forecast, you predict.

The Weather

Name:

Wednesday

Humidity

Temperature

. is moisture in the air.

tells how hot or cold it is.

When both are low, it's cool and dry.

The Weather

Name:

Thursday

barometer

thermometer

A barometer measures air pressure.

A thermometer measures temperature.

Name: _____

Extreme Weather

Sometimes weather can be extreme. A blizzard
is a bad snowstorm. Hurricanes, tornadoes,
and cyclones are violent windstorms.
A tsunami is a great sea wave. When
water overflows and covers the land,
it is called a flood.

Friday

Copy the paragraph.

EMC 793 • ©2000 by Evan-Moor Corp.

Our Presidents

Name:

Monday

George Washington

Washington was the first president.

He was a general in the army.

Our Presidents

Name:

Tuesday

Thomas Jefferson

Jefferson could speak five languages. He

wrote the Declaration of Independence.

Our Presidents

Name:

Wednesday

Abraham Lincoln

Lincoln was a Civil War president.

He signed a paper that freed slaves.

Our Presidents

Name:

Thursday

John F. Kennedy

Kennedy founded the Peace Corps.

He was assassinated in Dallas, Texas.

Name: _____

Friday

Presidential Oath of Office

I do solemnly swear that I will faithfully execute the office of President of the United States, and will, to the best of my ability, preserve, protect, and defend the Constitution of the United States.

Copy the oath.

Name:

Monday

Tic-Tac-Toe

three-in-a-row

Tic-Tac-Toe has many versions.

Three-in-a-row wins around the world.

Name:

Tuesday

Three Men's Morris

Three Men's Morris is an old game.

It was played in China in 1400 B.C.

Games Around the World

Wednesday

Seega

Egypt

Ancient Egyptians played Seega.

Players moved markers on a board.

Games Around the World

Name:

Thursday

Picaria

Native American

Players take turns placing markers.

They line up three markers to win.

Name: _____

Friday

Achi

Central African children draw the Achi game board in the dirt and gather small stones to use as markers. Copy the directions for play. Then try the game.

You Need:
• 2 players
• 8 markers:
  4 light-colored
  4 dark-colored
• game board

How to Play:

1. Take turns putting one marker at a time on any circle.

2. Try to get three markers in a row.

3. If no one gets three in a row, take turns moving the markers.

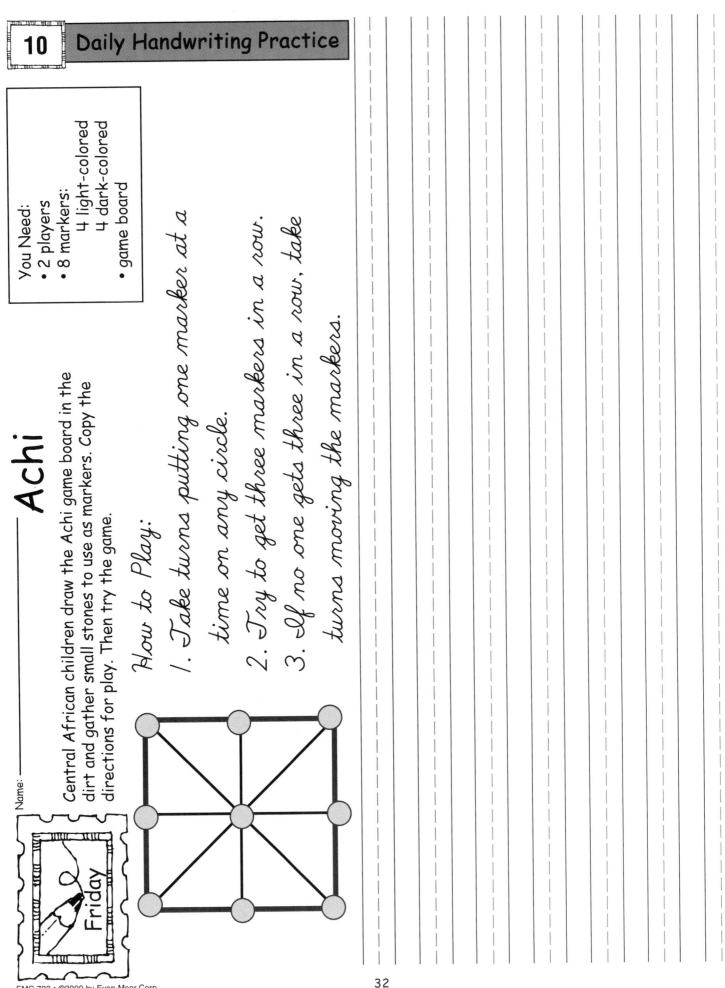

Name:

Monday

Onondaga

Seneca

Woodland tribes made homes of wood.

These natives lived by the water.

Name:

Tuesday

Pawnee

Sioux

Great Plains tribes tracked buffalo.

Their portable tents were easy to move.

Name:

Wednesday

Navajo

Pima

Zuni

These tribes were farmers and artists.

They made rugs, pottery, and jewelry.

Name:

Thursday

Kwakiutl

Nootka

These tribes built plank homes.

They held parties called potlatches.

Name:

Friday

Native Americans Yesterday and Today

Several million people lived in North
America before Europeans arrived.
Today reservations are located in
thirty-four states. Many Native
Americans live on these reservations.
Other Native Americans live in cities
and towns.

Copy the paragraph.

Name:

Monday

Venus'-flytrap

carnivorous

The Venus'-flytrap eats insects.

Its leaves work like a trap.

Name:

Tuesday

kapok tree

rainforest

The kapok tree can be 200 feet tall.

Many plants and animals live in it.

Name:

Wednesday

saguaro cactus

Sonoran Desert

The saguaro can be 200 years old.

Its skin stores rainwater.

Name:

Thursday

kelp

seaweed

The giant kelp is like a tree.

Its holdfast ties the plant to a rock.

Name: _____

Friday

Unusual Plants

There are many different kinds of plants. Each plant is adapted to the environment where it grows.

The Venus'-flytrap grows in an environment of limited nutrients so it has become carnivorous. The kapok tree has large palmlike leaves. The saguaro cactus has spiny needles. The kelp plant has a holdfast instead of a root.

Copy the paragraph.

Name:

Monday

un

tri

unhappy

tricycle

A prefix is at the beginning of a word.

re

pre

reopen

preview

Name:

Tuesday

im

dis

· imperfect

· ineffective

Add in or im to make an antonym.

· im

· mis

· disrespect

misprint

Prefixes & Suffixes

Name:

Wednesday

ful

by

en

ology

hopeful

quickly

wooden

biology

Put a suffix at the end of a word.

Prefixes & Suffixes

Name:

Thursday

less

ment

movement

agreement

hopeless

careless

"without"

The suffix less means without.

40

Name: _____

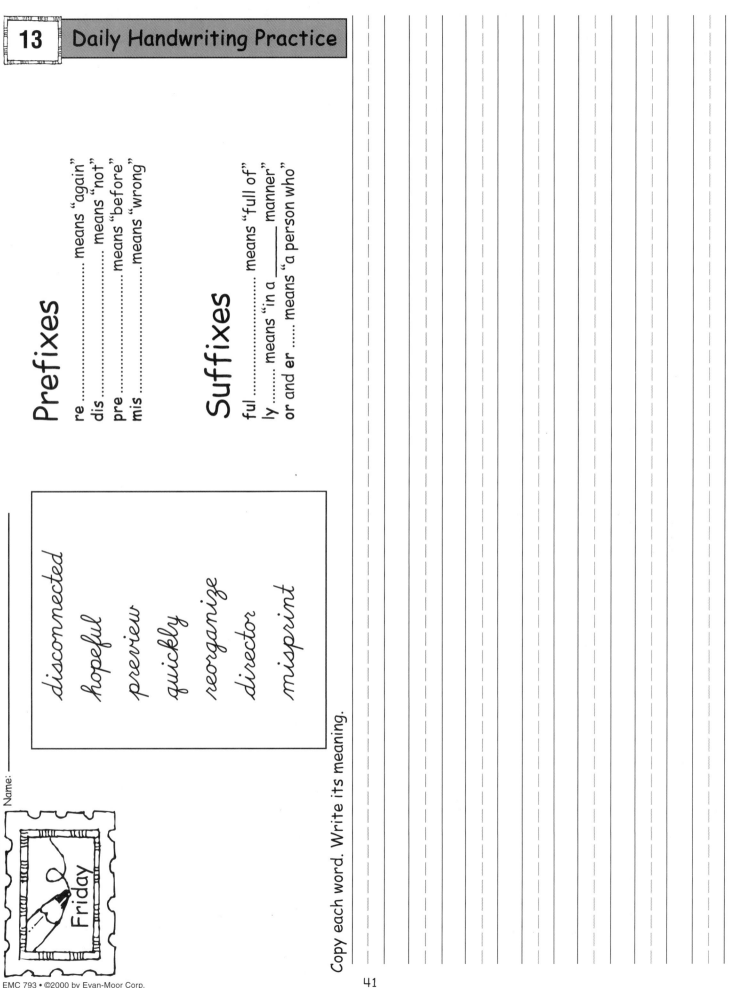

Friday

Prefixes

re .... means "again"
dis .... means "not"
pre .... means "before"
mis .... means "wrong"

Suffixes

ful .... means "full of"
ly .... means "in a ____ manner"
or and er ..... means "a person who"

disconnected

hopeful

preview

quickly

reorganize

director

misprint

Copy each word. Write its meaning.

Rhyming Words

Name:

Monday

spoon

balloon

moon

noon

You seldom see the moon at noon.

Try to pop a balloon with a spoon.

Rhyming Words

Name:

Tuesday

bug

slug

rug

hug

He is as snug as a bug in a rug.

It would be hard to hug a slug.

Rhyming Words

Name:

drink

wrink

think

shrink

Wednesday

Can you drink while you wrink?

Will you shrink? Do you think?

Rhyming Words

Name:

freeze

sneeze

trapeze

freeze

Thursday

When you're on a trapeze,

it's a bad time to sneeze.

Name: _____

Rhyming Riddles

Answer each riddle
with a rhyming pair.

dinosaur carnivore   lucky ducky

redhead   green bean

marriage carriage   flat hat

big pig

Someone whose hair is the color of a rose

redhead

A large hog

_____

A cap after the elephant sat on it

_____

A vegetable that grows on a vine

_____

A web-footed winner

_____

The wagon used by the bride and groom

_____

A prehistoric creature that eats meat

_____

Friday

Rivers of the World

Name:

Monday

Amazon

Madeira

Japura

Purus

Many rivers flow into the Amazon.

They are called tributaries.

Rivers of the World

Name:

Tuesday

Mississippi

Rio Grande

Mackenzie

Colorado

St. Lawrence

The Mississippi is Old Man River.

Name:

Wednesday

Thames

Volga

Seine

Rhine

The Thames flows through London.

The Rhine was important in history.

Name:

Thursday

Yangtze

Euphrates

Tigris

Ganges

The Yangtze is a very long river.

Chinese civilization began along it.

Name: _____

Rivers of the World
Africa

Nile

The Nile is the longest river in the world. The name Nile came from the Greek word "neilos," which means "valley." Water from the river and fertile soil along its banks made this river valley a good place for ancient peoples to live and farm.

Copy the paragraph.

EMC 793 • ©2000 by Evan-Moor Corp.

Nonsense Rhymes

Name:

Monday

Down by the river,

Down by the sea,

Kitty went fishing with kittens three.

Nonsense Rhymes

Name:

Tuesday

Johnny's over the ocean.

Johnny's over the sea.

Johnny broke a cup and he blamed me.

Name:

Wednesday

Mama, Mama, I am sick.

Send for the doctor,

Quick, quick, quick!

Nonsense Rhymes

Name:

Thursday

Cinderella dressed in red

Went inside to bake some bread.

How many loaves did Cinderella bake?

Name: _____

Friday

Nonsense Rhymes Fun

Bubble gum, bubble gum,

chew and blow.

Bubble gum, bubble gum,

scrape your toe.

Bubble gum, bubble gum,

tastes so sweet.

Get that bubble gum off your feet!

Copy the rhyme.

Name:

Monday

silky anteater

howler monkey

The eats ants.

The 's roar is loud.

Unusual Animals

Name:

Tuesday

atelopus

gecko

The atelopus is a poisonous frog.

The gecko has suction cups on its feet.

Unusual Animals

Name:

Wednesday

black agouti

crab spider

The agouti cracks nuts with its jaws.

The crab spider looks like a flower.

Unusual Animals

Name:

Thursday

Hercules beetle

toucan

The Hercules beetle is 6 inches long.

The toucan's large beak is not heavy.

Name: _____

Friday

In a Tropical Rainforest

Imagine walking through a rainforest...

Rain drips from the tips of leaves.
Frogs croak and monkeys cry
As giant butterflies quietly pass by.
Imagine standing on the forest floor...
Look up through the understory.
Look past the thick canopy
To the emergent layer and the sky.

Imagine walking through a rainforest...

Copy the poem.

Owls Are Amazing Hunters

Name:

Monday

keen ears

sharp eyes

An owl can see even when it is dark.

An owl can hear animals moving.

Owls Are Amazing Hunters

Name:

Tuesday

sharp talons

hunters

An owl has four talons on each foot.

An owl uses its talons to grab a meal.

Owls Are Amazing Hunters

Name:

Wednesday

fringed

feathers

The owl has fringed feathers.

The feathers help the owl fly quietly.

Thursday

no teeth

swallows

An owl tears its food apart.

It even swallows the bones.

55

Name: _____

Friday

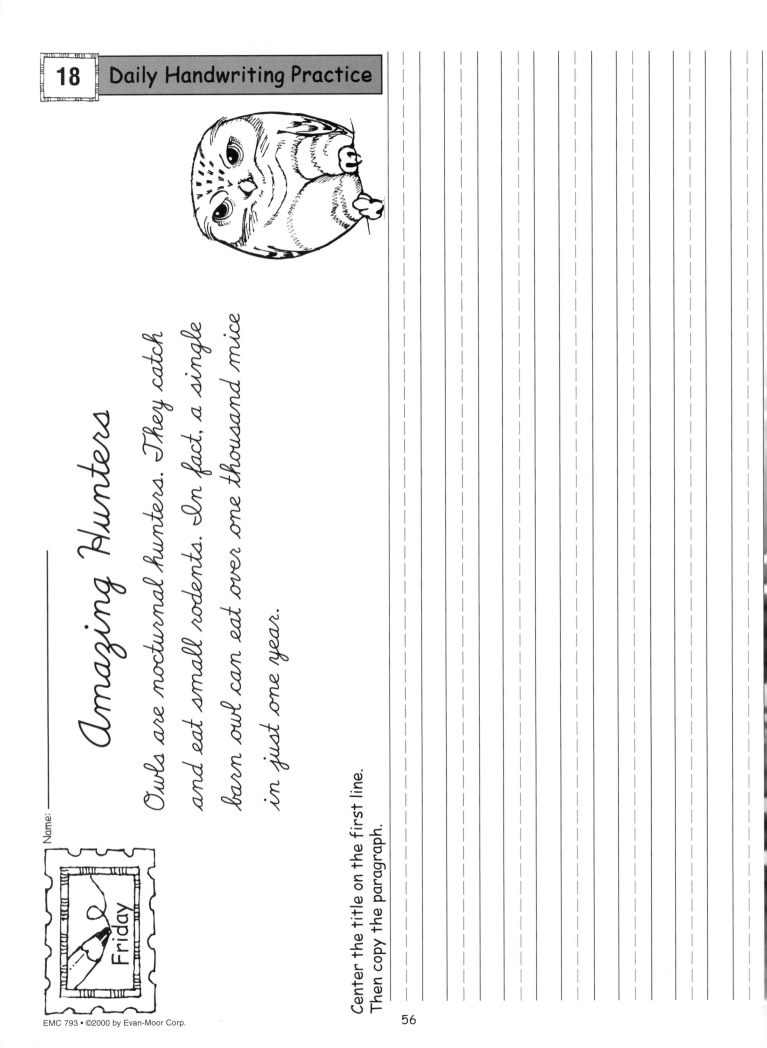

Amazing Hunters

Owls are nocturnal hunters. They catch and eat small rodents. In fact, a single barn owl can eat over one thousand mice in just one year.

Center the title on the first line.
Then copy the paragraph.

Whales

Whales

Whales have blowholes.

Monday

The holes are on top of their heads.

Whales use their blowholes to breathe.

Name:

A whale swims to the surface.

Tuesday

It makes a spout called a blow.

The blow is droplets of water and air.

Whales

Name:

Wednesday

It closes its blowhole and dives.

It can hold its breath underwater.

A whale surfaces, blows, and dives.

Whales

Name:

Thursday

Whales blow differently.

Some whales have one blowhole.

Some whales have two blowholes.

Name: _____

Friday

Know Your Blows

The blue whale's blow is narrow and high.
Right whales make two low blows with their
twin blowholes. The humpback whale has a
low blow. The sperm whale makes a blow
that is angled forward and to the left.

Copy the facts.

The Water Cycle

Name:

Monday

water vapor

invisible gas

Air around us is filled with water.

Hot water changes into water vapor.

The Water Cycle

Name:

Tuesday

droplet

cool

breath

warm

When water vapor cools, it forms drops.

Cold air changes the vapor into droplets.

The Water Cycle

Name:

Wednesday

gas

vapor

liquid

droplets

Droplets are liquid. Vapor is gas.

Water changes its form over and over.

The Water Cycle

Name:

Thursday

condensation

evaporation

Condensation = water vapor to droplets.

Evaporation = water droplets to vapor.

Name: _____

Friday

The Water Cycle

Hot sun warms the Earth. The heat causes water to evaporate. The water vapor rises into the sky and meets cold air. It condenses into droplets. Millions of drops come together to make clouds. When a cloud gets full of water, waterdrops fall back to Earth.

Copy the paragraph.

The Months of the Year

January

February

January is named after a Roman god.

Janus was the god of all beginnings.

March

April

Monday

Name:

May

June

In Canada, Dominion Day is July 1.

U.S. Independence Day is July 4.

July

August

Tuesday

Name:

Wednesday

September

October

November

December

These names come from Latin words.

Name:

Thursday

Winter

Spring

Summer

Autumn

The year is divided into four seasons.

64

Name:

Friday

Months of the Year

Thirty days hath September,
April, June, and November;
All the rest have thirty-one,
Excepting February alone,
And that has twenty-eight days clear
And twenty-nine in each leap year.

Copy this traditional verse.

Using Good Verbs

Name:

Monday

whispered

shouted

The cheerleader _____ "Yea!"

The librarian _____ "Quiet!"

Using Good Verbs

Name:

Tuesday

plodded

crept

The mouse _____ home.

The elephant _____ home.

Using Good Verbs

Name:

Wednesday

dozed

napped

The cuddly kitten .

The tired puppy .

Using Good Verbs

Name:

Thursday

scribbled

jotted

The man the message.

The child the message.

Name: _____

Friday

Poets Use Good Verbs

Copy this portion of the poem *Jump or Jiggle* by Evelyn Beyer.

Worms wiggle

Bugs jiggle

Puppies bounce

Kittens pounce

Lions stalk

But I walk!

Figures of Speech

Name:

Monday

simile

like   as

A simile uses the words like or as.

The boy ate like a starved animal.

Figures of Speech

Name:

Tuesday

metaphor

comparison

A metaphor doesn't use like or as.

Her voice was a symphony of sounds.

Figures of Speech

Name:

Wednesday

personification

human traits

Personification makes things human.

My bike cried as I skidded to a stop.

Figures of Speech

Name:

Thursday

alliteration

repetition

Alliteration is the repetition of sounds.

Suddenly soapy suds swallowed a sock.

Name: _____

Friday

Copy each example of figurative language by its name.

His voice is as round and strong as a canyon echo.

from *Song and Dance Man* by Karen Ackerman

I could almost see the moon, with a can of paint, spraying the black water.

from *Whale Brother* by Barbara Steiner

Fire is a dragon alive in the night;
Fiery dragon, glittering bright.

from *Fire* by Shirley Hughes

Peter Piper picked a peck of pickled peppers.

from *Mother Goose*

simile

_____

_____

metaphor

_____

_____

alliteration

_____

_____

personification

_____

_____

Colors and Alliteration

Name:

Monday

red

blue

rose

blossom

A riot of red roses rings the rock.

blue blossoms, a blooming blanket

Colors and Alliteration

Name:

Tuesday

white

gray

whiskers

grout

Which whisker is the white whisker?

Grandpa ground a groove in the grout.

Colors and Alliteration

Name:

Wednesday

purple

pink

peacocks

peony

Peacocks paraded in purple plumes.

Pink peony posed for a portrait.

Colors and Alliteration

Name:

Thursday

yellow

green

yolks

grass

Yesterday's yolks were yucky yellow.

Greedy groundhogs grab green grass.

Name: _____

Friday

A Cold, Cold Day

On my cold, cold toes are yellow socks.

On my cold, cold hands are blue gloves.

On my cold, cold head is a tall red cap.

On my cold, cold back is a soft tan coat.

On my cold, cold legs are purple sweats.

On my cold, cold nose is an icicle!

Copy the sentences. Then draw and color a picture on the back of the paper.

Name:

Monday

Beavers

habitat

Beavers change their habitats.

They block up streams to make ponds.

Name:

Tuesday

Beavers are good swimmers.

Muscles keep water out of their noses.

See-through eyelids act like goggles.

Name:

Wednesday

lodges

hollow

Beavers build a hollow lodge.

It has an underwater entrance.

Name:

Thursday

Beavers build dams.

They put stones on top of branches.

They scoop mud to fill in the spaces.

Name: _____

Friday

A Beaver's Tale

The beaver's broad tail acts like a rudder to steer when it swims. Its webbed back feet help it swim. Strong front paws help it dig and carry. Two very large orange front teeth gnaw down trees. All in all, the beaver is perfectly equipped to be a pond engineer.

Copy the paragraph.

Name:

Monday

Machines

Simple machines

Machines make our work easier.

Simple machines are in all machines.

Name:

Tuesday

lever

pulley

A lever is a bar used for lifting.

A pulley makes it easier to move stuff.

Simple Machines

Name:

Wednesday

screw

wedge

A screw can move things up and down.

A wedge is used to cut or split things.

Simple Machines

Name:

Thursday

wheel and axle

inclined plane

When a wheel turns, the axle turns.

An inclined plane is a tilted surface.

Name: _____

Friday

What Is Work?

Write *work* or *not work* below each task.
Remember there must be a force and movement.

work

not work

Scientists say that work is done if a push or force is used to move something over a distance. If the thing doesn't move, it is not considered work.

Copy the paragraph.

Name:

Monday

"Listen, my children, and you shall hear
of the midnight ride of Paul Revere....One
if by land, and two, if by sea....."

H. W. Longfellow from *Paul Revere's Ride*

Famous Quotations

Name:

Tuesday

"I must go down to the seas again, to the
lonely sea and the sky, And all I ask is a
tall ship and a star to steer her by."

John Masefield from *Sea Fever*

Famous Quotations

Famous Quotations

Name:

Wednesday

"They have yarns of a skyscraper so tall that they had to put hinges on the top two stories so to let the moon go by."

Carl Sandburg from *They Have Yarns*

Name:

Thursday

"Where we walk to school each day Indian children used to play...All about our Native land, where the shops and houses stand."

Annette Wynne from *Indian Children*

Famous Quotations

Name: _____

Friday

"Whose woods these are I think I know.

His house is in the village though;

He will not see me stopping here

To watch his woods fill up with snow....

The woods are lovely, dark and deep

But I have promises to keep,

And miles to go before I sleep...."

Robert Frost from *Stopping By Woods on a Snowy Evening*

Copy the poem.

Name:

Monday

sports

games

physical activity

Kids around the world play sports.

Sports are organized games.

Name:

Tuesday

soccer

football

kick

goal

The most popular sport is soccer.

In most places, soccer is called football.

Name:

Malaysia

footbag

Sepak raga is played in Malaysia.

Players pass a footbag to each other.

Wednesday

Sports Around the World

Name:

Tennis

France

Tennis probably originated in France.

It was played with a gloved hand.

Thursday

Name:

Friday

The Olympics

The first Olympic Games were held in Olympus, Greece, in 776 B.C. Today's Olympic competitions include many different sports. Approximately 10,200 athletes participated in the 2000 Summer Games in Australia.

Copy the paragraph.

Name:

Monday

sugar

candy

sweet tooth

Do you have a sweet tooth?

yes or no

Do you like all kinds of candy?

yes or no

The word *candy* comes from the Arabic word for *sugar.*

Candy Around the World

Name:

Tuesday

Switzerland

Belgium

Many candies are made out of chocolate.

Switzerland and Belgium are famous for their chocolates.

Carob is a substitute for chocolate.

Name:

Italy

Wednesday

Middle East

Italian children like chewy nougats.

Middle Eastern children like halvah.

Halvah is a sesame honey candy.

Name:

Seker Bayrami

Thursday

Turkish Delight

Seker Bayrami is a candy holiday.

It is celebrated in Turkey.

MMMmmm Candy Marbles!!

Friday

What You Need:
1/2 cup chunky peanut butter
1/4 cup evaporated milk
1/4 cup brown sugar
1 teaspoon cinnamon
1 cup crispy chow mein noodles, slightly crushed
1 cup stick pretzels, slightly crushed
1/2 cup chopped nuts

What You Do:

1. Stir the peanut butter, evaporated milk,
   brown sugar, and cinnamon together.
   Cook for five minutes.
2. Stir in noodles, pretzels, and nuts.
3. Drop spoonfuls onto a cookie sheet.
4. Chill for one hour.
5. Pop one in your mouth!

Copy the steps for making Candy Marbles.

Name:

Monday

Africa

Kenya

equator

Kenya is on the east coast of Africa.

Kenya lies across the equator.

Name:

Tuesday

Nairobi

Swahili

Nairobi is the capital city of Kenya.

The people speak Swahili or English.

Wednesday

Masai Mara

game park

Wild animals are safe in Masai Mara.

Many animals live in the game park.

Learning About Kenya

Name:

Thursday

Mombasa

harbor

Kenya's second-largest city is Mombasa.

Mombasa has a very busy harbor.

Kenya's Flag

Name: _____

Friday

The flag of Kenya has three stripes on it. The top stripe is black. The center stripe is red and the bottom stripe is green. The red stripe in the center is edged in white. In the middle of the flag there is a Masai warrior's shield with two crossed spears.

The black on the flag represents the people of Kenya. The red represents the blood shed in Kenya's fight for independence. The green represents the fertility of the land. The white represents peace. The shield of the warrior represents Kenya's pride and tradition.

Copy the paragraph.

Monday

addition.

subtraction.

Add two numbers to get a sum.

Subtract to get the difference.

Writing About Math

Name:

Tuesday

multiplication.

division.

Multiply to get the product.

Divide to find the quotient.

Name:

Wednesday

Mathematics

Arithmetic

Mathematics is the science of numbers.

Arithmetic is part of mathematics.

Name:

Thursday

geometry

algebra

There are different kinds of math.

What kind is your favorite?

Name: _____

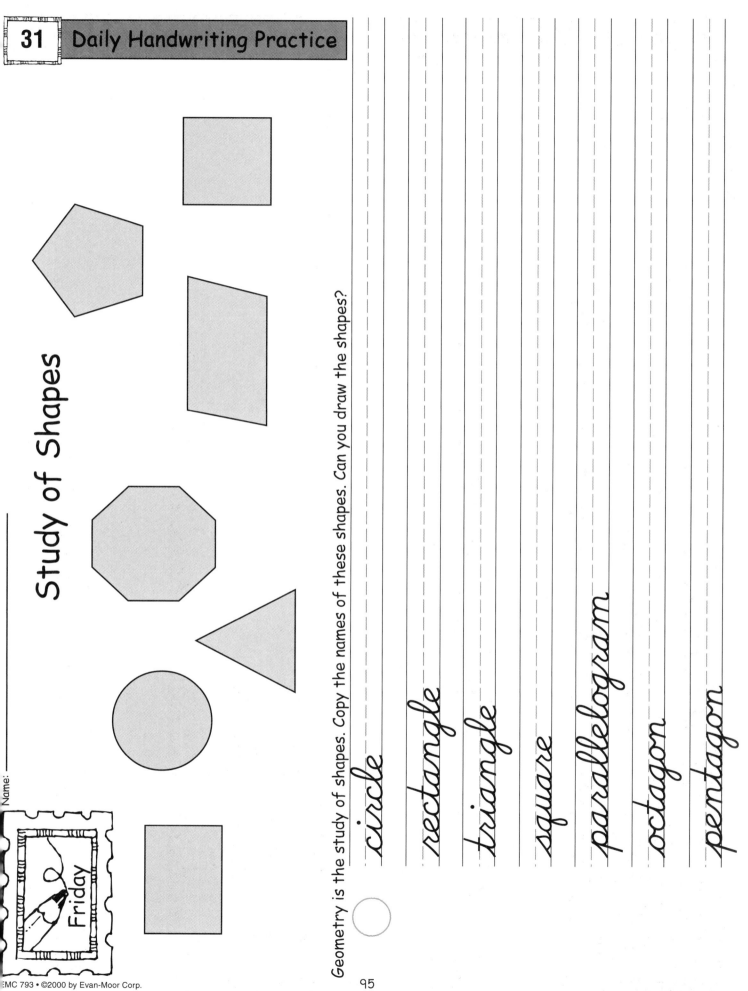

Study of Shapes

Geometry is the study of shapes. Copy the names of these shapes. Can you draw the shapes?

circle

rectangle

triangle

square

parallelogram

octagon

pentagon

32 Daily Handwriting Practice

Name:

Monday

alphabet

Roman

The Roman alphabet has 26 letters.

Alphabet letters represent sounds.

32 Daily Handwriting Practice

Name:

Tuesday

Chinese writing uses characters.

Characters stand for words and ideas.

Today Chinese students learn pin-yin.

Name:

Wednesday

There are different alphabets.

The Arabic alphabet is used in Egypt.

It's used to write Arabic and Kurdish.

Alphabets Around the World

Name:

Thursday

Thai alphabet

Asia

It has symbols for different vowels.

It is used throughout Asia.

Name: _____

Hooray for Cyril and Methodius!

Friday

In the late ninth century, two Greek brothers named Cyril and Methodius revised and refined the Greek alphabet. The alphabet was a great success. Today it is called the Cyrillic alphabet. It is used to write Bulgarian, Russian, and a number of other Slavic languages.

Copy the paragraph.

Buggy Alphabet

Name:

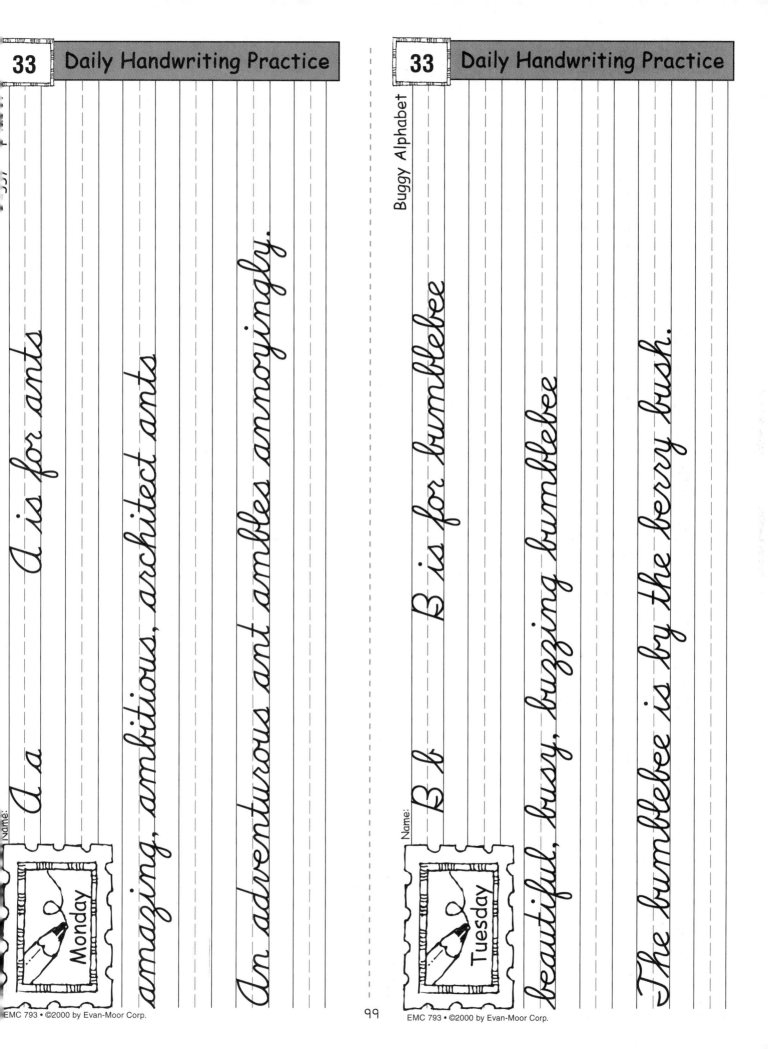

A a

A is for ants

Monday

amazing, ambitious, architect ants

An adventurous ant ambles annoyingly.

Name:

B b

B is for bumblebee

Tuesday

beautiful, busy, buzzing bumblebee

The bumblebee is by the berry bush.

Name:

Wednesday

Cc

C is for crickets

cheerful, chirping cricket chorus

Crickets, creep up. Commence chirping.

Name:

Thursday

Dd

D is for damselfly

dainty, demure, darting damselfly

Don't disturb the delicate damselfly.

Buggy Alphabet

Name:

Friday

E e

E is for earring

enormous, exotic, excitable earring

The earring excavates an earthen nest.

Buggy Alphabet

F f

F is for fleas

formidable, flourishing fleas

Fumigate a fast-growing family of fleas.

Buggy Alphabet

Name:

Monday

Gg

G is for grasshoppers

great, gravity-defying grasshoppers

Green grasshoppers gracefully glide.

Buggy Alphabet

Name:

Tuesday

Hh

H is for housefly

hovering, hungry, harassing housefly

Hurry, help me hit that housefly!

102

Buggy Alphabet

Name:

Wednesday

I i

I is for inchworm

itty-bitty, industrious inchworm

Imagine inching innocently forward.

Buggy Alphabet

Name:

Thursday

J j

J is for June beetle

Just a jet-setting June beetle

June beetle journeys on jaunty wings.

Buggy Alphabet

Name:

K k

K is for katydid

kind, kinetic katydid

Katydid keeps on key as it sings.

Friday

Buggy Alphabet

L l

L is for ladybug

lovely, little ladybug

Ladybug lifts its wings and launches.

Buggy Alphabet

Name:

M m

M is for mosquitoes

maddening, marauding mosquitoes

Mash the menacing mob of mosquitoes.

Monday

Name:

N n

N is for nightcrawlers

ninety nocturnal nightcrawlers

Nightcrawlers never nap as they nibble.

Tuesday

Buggy Alphabet

Name:

Wednesday

O o

O is for oriental cockroach

overbold, objectionable cockroach

Oriental cockroach outruns homeowners.

Buggy Alphabet

Name:

Thursday

P p

P is for praying mantis

peculiar, patient praying mantis

Praying mantis poses on its perch.

Name:

Friday

2 q

2 is for queen termite

quiet, quivering queen termite

Quickly the queen lays eggs.

Buggy Alphabet

R r

R is for rhinoceros beetle

really robust rhinoceros beetle

Regardless of rain, it rambles.

Buggy Alphabet

Buggy Alphabet

Name:

Name:

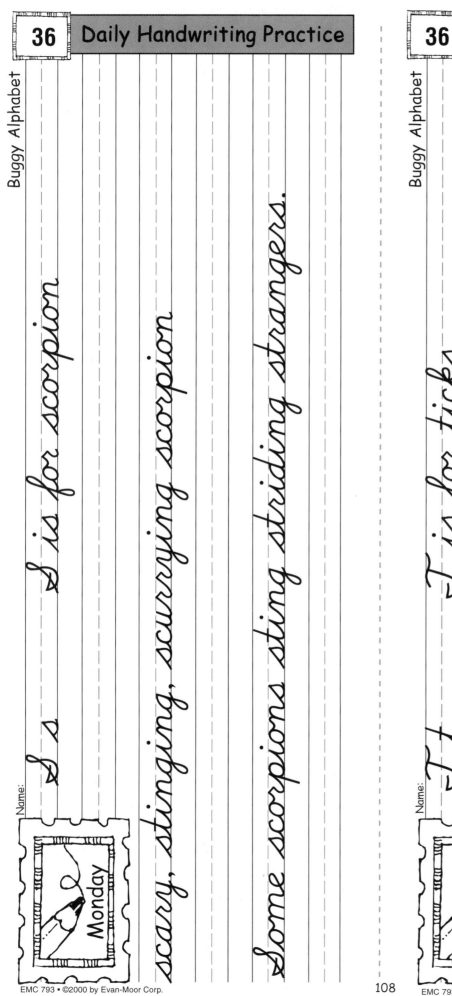

S s

S is for scorpion

scary, stinging, scurrying scorpion

Some scorpions sting striding strangers.

Monday

T t

T is for ticks

tailless, troublesome ticks

Ticks target tempting, tasty tourists.

Tuesday

Wednesday

U u

U is for underwing moth

unique, unusual underwing moth

Usually the underwing uses its wings.

Buggy Alphabet

Name:

Thursday

V v

V is for velvet ants

very vulnerable velvet ants

Velvet ants rely on their velveteen coats.

Velvet ants are really flightless female digger wasps.

Name:

W w

W is for water strider

water-skiing water strider

Its widespread legs walk on water.

Friday

X x

X is for xylophanes tersa

excellent sphinx moth

Xylophanes tersa is a sphinx moth.

Name:

Y y

Y is for yellow jacket

Y

y

Friday

Yikes! It's a yellow jacket.

Yellow jackets think you are yummy.

Buggy Alphabet

Z z

Z is for zebra swallowtail

Z

Z

Zipping, zooming zebra swallowtail

Zebra swallowtails zigzag with zeal.

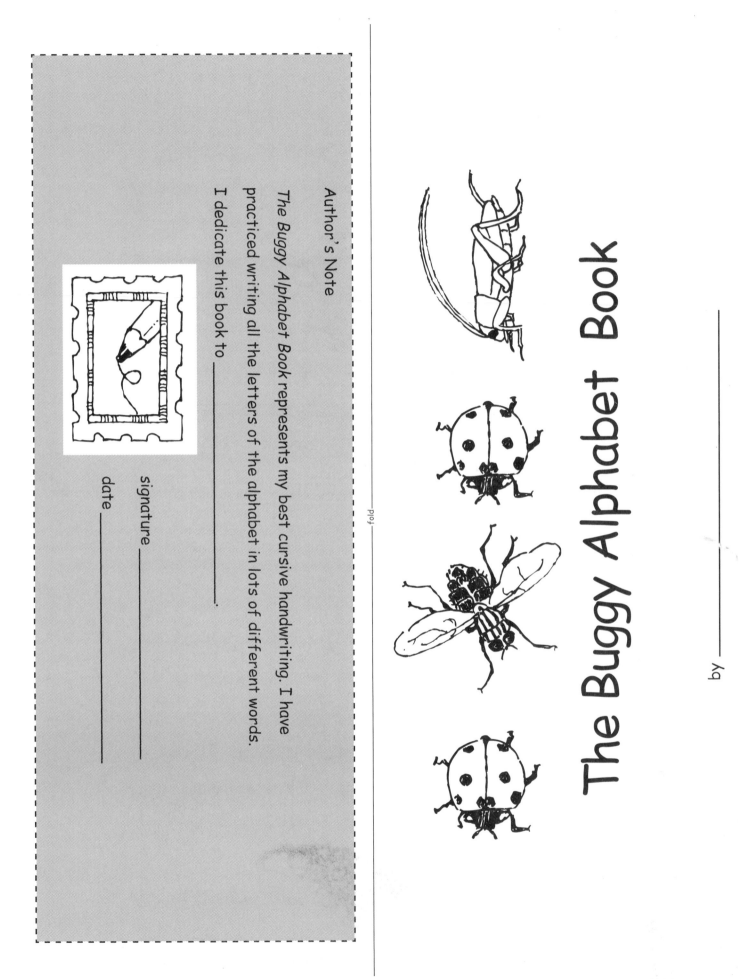

The Buggy Alphabet Book

by _____

Author's Note

The *Buggy Alphabet Book* represents my best cursive handwriting. I have practiced writing all the letters of the alphabet in lots of different words.

I dedicate this book to

_____.

_____
signature

_____
date

fold

112